FRANKLIN SCHOOL
LIBRARY MEDIA CENTER

W9-CHN-001

MARCO POLO

EXPEDITION

A JOURNEY THROUGH CHINA

Editor April McCroskie

An SBC Book, created, designed, and produced by
The Salariya Book Company Ltd
25 Marlborough Place
Brighton
United Kingdom

© The Salariya Book Company Limited MCMXCVII

First published in 1997 by Franklin Watts
96 Leonard Street London EC2A 4RH

First American edition 1998 by
Franklin Watts
A Division of Grolier Publishing
Sherman Turnpike
Danbury, CT 06816

10 9 8 7 6 5 4 3 2 1

ISBN: 0-531-14453-4

Printed in Singapore

Library of Congress Cataloging-in-Publication Data
Macdonald, Fiona.
Marco Polo: a journey through China / written by Fiona Macdonald ;
illustrated by Mark Bergin ; created and designed by David Salariya. --
1st American ed.
    p. cm. -- (Expedition)
Includes index.
Summary: Describes Marco Polo's travels through Asia, and discusses
the people and cultures he encountered.
ISBN 0-531-14453-4
 1.Polo, Marco, 1254-1323?--Journeys--Juvenile literature. 2. Voyages and
travels--Juvenile literature. 3. Explorers--Italy-Biography-Juvenile literature. 4. China--Description and travel-Juvenile literature. (1. Polo, Marco,
1254-1323? 2. Explorers. 3. Asia--Description and travel.) I. Bergin, Mark,
ill. II. Salariya, David. III. Title. IV. Series.
G370. P9M355 1998
915. 104'25'092--dc2
  (B)   97-7533
                                                               CIP AC

MARCO POLO
A Journey through China

Written by FIONA MACDONALD

Illustrated by MARK BERGIN

Created and designed by
DAVID SALARIYA

FRANKLIN SCHOOL
LIBRARY MEDIA CENTER

W

FRANKLIN WATTS
A Division of Grolier Publishing
NEW YORK • LONDON • HONG KONG • SYDNEY
DANBURY, CONNECTICUT

CONTENTS

INTRODUCTION

MARCO POLO was born in Italy, in 1254. When he died in 1324, aged 70, he could look back on a lifetime of extraordinary adventures, traveling across half the known world in the service of the formidable Mongol emperor, Kublai Khan.

On his journeys, Marco Polo explored rich cities and fabulous palaces, admired spectacular scenery, and met fascinating local peoples. None had been seen by Europeans before.

Marco Polo had his amazing adventures written down. If this book is true – and scholars think it probably is – he traveled farther, and saw more, than anyone ever before.

THE MONGOL PEACE

Although Marco Polo faced many dangers on his journeys, he lived at a time when travel across Asia was safe – at least by medieval standards. This was because the Mongols, fierce nomad soldiers led by warrior Chingiz Khan (died 1227), had conquered a vast empire, stretching from Turkey to China. The Mongols were ruthless invaders, but they brought law and order to the lands they ruled.

Fine New Buildings
St Mark's cathedral (rebuilt and extended in the 13th century) was one of the many new buildings in Marco Polo's Venice. It was filled with treasures, looted in 1207 from the rich city of Constantinople (present-day Istanbul).

A City by the Sea
Venice was built on a cluster of islands, linked by bridges, in a shallow, marshy lagoon. There was a long waterfront, right in the city center, where ships could unload their cargoes ready for eager merchants to buy.

MARCO POLO was born in Venice – a rich, proud, powerful city in northern Italy. Venice was a port and its wealth came from trade. Like many other Venetian citizens, Marco Polo's family were merchants, making a living by buying and selling goods.

Sailing ships from countries all round the Mediterranean Sea docked in the lagoon – Venice's shallow, sheltered harbor. They were loaded with valuable cargoes from distant lands. Venice was also the major port for ships sailing to Europe from the Black Sea.

Traders bargained to get the best prices for goods they had brought from overseas.

1   2   3   4   5   6

You could find all these goods on sale in Marco Polo's Venice:
Intricate Glassware
1. Glass mosque lamp, from Syria.
2. Glass beaker, from Venice.

Brilliant Glazes
3. Glazed pottery tile, made in Kushan, Iraq.
4. Pottery bowl and plate with an intricate pattern, from Iran.

Fine Metalware
5. Inlaid bronze oil-lamp shaped like a jug, made in Iran.
6. Brass and silver ewer (water jug), made in Syria.

Shops and Streets

The city streets of Venice were lined with market stalls. There were also booths where bankers, money-changers, and money-lenders did business. Rich merchants had shops and showrooms in their own homes.

The Polos' Home

The Polos' family home in Venice is shown above. Only rich merchants could afford houses like this. It was built on several floors, with doorways and windows decorated with the latest designs.

Rich merchants' houses were spacious, and well-heated. They had tapestry wall-hangings, rush mats, and carved wooden chests. Light came from beeswax candles. Merchants often entertained customers in their homes. If they enjoyed their visit, they might buy more!

7

8

9

10

Chinese Ceramics

7. Stoneware (pottery) pillow, decorated with Chinese characters and chrysanthemum flowers, made in China in 1071.

Porcelain

8. Decorated porcelain box with a celadon (green) glaze.
9. Eight-sided porcelain vase, with a bluish-green glaze, made in China around 1200.

Bronze

10. Ornate bronze vase, designed to stand on a wealthy family's household altar and hold flowers, made in China around 1300.

Silk and Wool
Left: Silk with a pattern of lions, woven in Turkey around 1230.
Right: Woolen carpet with a geometric pattern, made for a mosque in Konya, Turkey, in the early 14th century.

Exotic Spices
Favorite spices imported into Europe from India and the Spice Islands:
1. Ginger 2. Nutmeg
3. Mace 4. Black pepper
5. Cloves 6. Cinnamon.

Merchants liked to wear fashionable clothes.

VALUABLE GOODS from the Far East reached European ports, like Venice, by two different routes. The "Silk Road" ran overland, from China to the shores of the Black Sea. The "Spice Route" stretched across the sea from China and the Spice Islands (in present-day Indonesia), then over the Indian Ocean to the Red Sea and the Persian Gulf.

Few traders traveled all the way along the Silk Road or the Spice Route. Instead, they made purchases from merchants in neighboring lands. Goods were often bought and sold several times on their long international journeys by land and sea.

Silk-making in China
Silk-making was a closely-guarded secret.
1. Silkworm Moth Eggs
Eggs were collected, left to hatch into grubs, and fed with mulberry leaves.

2. Worms at Work
Mature silkworms were arranged on racks. At this stage of their life cycle, the worms were ready to spin cocoons of fine, silky thread.

3. Boiling Water
When the silkworms had finished spinning, the cocoons were dropped in boiling water to soften them and loosen the fibers.

•THE SILK ROAD AND THE SPICE ROUTE•

Long Journey
Goods were carried overland along the Silk Road by pack-horses, mules, or camels, until they reached trading ports on the shores of the Black Sea. Then they were loaded onto ships, to complete the journey to Venice.

Barter and Exchange
Craftworkers and merchants living in different countries used different currencies, and were often suspicious of each other's coins. So many goods were exchanged for food, horses, or other valuable items, instead.

This map shows the Silk Road and the Spice Route. Travelers making long journeys often had to pay high tolls to local rulers before being allowed to continue their journey. They added these charges to the price of the goods they were carrying, making them even more expensive.

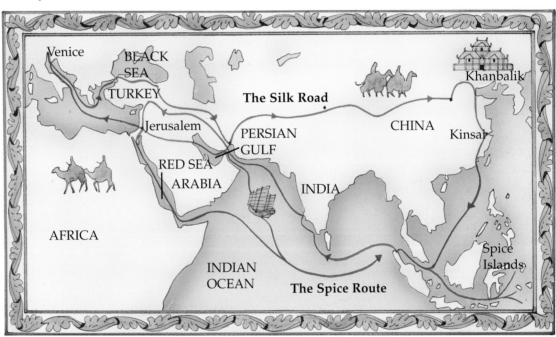

4. Unwinding Cocoons
The cocoons were unwound carefully by hand. Each one yielded between 990 and 1650 yards (900 and 1500 meters) of delicate, shiny silk.

5. Making Thread
Several fine strands of silk were twisted together to make thicker threads, strong enough to be woven into cloth.

6. Weaving and Dyeing
The threads were woven on a simple hand-loom, then dyed in bright colors using mixtures of plants and crushed earth.

• MONGOL LORDS OF ASIA •

1. Off to China

The Polos sailed from Venice to Constantinople at the entrance to the Black Sea. Constantinople was a busy trading city. They would have met merchants from many Middle East countries in Constantinople's bustling bazaars.

2. From Europe to Asia

The next stage of the journey was by ship across the Black Sea to the important trading port of Sudak in the Crimea (present-day Ukraine). One of their brothers owned a shop there.

IN 1260, Marco Polo's father, Niccolo, and uncle, Maffeo, made a bold decision. They would travel East themselves, maybe to China, and stock up with valuable silks and jewels to sell when they returned home. The trip would be long and risky, but they hoped to make their fortunes this way.

The Polos' journey was longer than they had expected. They were away from home for almost nine years, trapped in Central Asia by a war between rival Mongol tribes. But they finally managed to reach China, where they met the mighty Mongol emperor, Kublai Khan. They returned home safely in 1268.

Kublai Khan gave the Polos a gold paitze (like a passport) so they could travel home safely.

Mongol Lifestyle

The Mongols were nomads who moved from place to place in search of food. They lived in big felt tents, called "yurts."

Nomad Foods

The Mongols kept herds of goats and sheep. They did not grow any crops or vegetables. Their main foods were meat and milk.

Clothes against the Cold

Mongol clothes were designed for warmth on bitterly-cold steppes (grasslands). Men and women wore long sheepskin coats, and trousers.

• THE OLDER POLOS MEET KUBLAI KHAN •

3. Merchant Cities
In the Central Asian city of Bukhara the Polos took refuge from the Mongols' civil war. They joined a group of merchants setting off for China and the court of Kublai Khan (ruled 1260-1294).

4. Meeting Kublai Khan
Finally, they reached the Mongols' capital city in China at Khanbalik (present-day Beijing). Armed guards took them to Kublai Khan's palace. But Kublai welcomed them. He was interested in Europeans.

The Mongols were brave fighters. They conquered an empire which stretched from Hungary to Korea.

Boots and Stirrups
1. Embroidered leather boots, worn by men and women.
2. Stirrups helped Mongols to fight better on horseback. They were skilled riders.

Milk Drink
The Mongols drank *kumiz*, a nourishing but very alcoholic drink made from mare's milk. It was stored in decorated flasks like these (*above*).

Mongol Entertainments
1. Finely-decorated, single-stringed fiddle.
2. Mongol game, played with bone counters on a wooden board.

•THE ADVENTURE BEGINS•

Sea Travel
Journeys by sea were hazardous in the Middle Ages. Travelers braved storms, shipwrecks, and attack by pirates. But for merchants and adventurers like the Polos, the financial rewards could be great.

Setting Sail
In 1271, the Polos sailed from Venice across the Mediterranean Sea. They arrived in Acre, a busy port in the Holy Land, just south of the present-day city of Beirut in Lebanon.

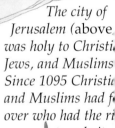

The city of Jerusalem (above) was holy to Christi... Jews, and Muslims Since 1095 Christi... and Muslims had f... over who had the ri... to rule it.

Niccolo and Maffeo Polo had promised Kublai Khan they would return. So in 1271 they set off again for China, taking seventeen-year-old Marco with them. For Marco, it was the start of a lifetime of adventure. He did not see his home again for over 20 years.

The first stage of the Polos' journey ended in Jerusalem, where they collected a flask of precious holy oil to take as a present to Kublai Khan. Then they headed east, traveling through wild countryside and admiring the prosperous towns and beautiful buildings they saw along the way.

Acre, Palestine
In Palestine the Polos hoped to find Christian missionaries willing to travel with them to China. But mostly, they only met traders and farmers.

The Holy Sepulcher
At the Holy Sepulcher (Jesus's tomb) in Jerusalem, the Polos collected holy oil from the lamp that was kept burning there continually.

Mount Ararat, Armenia
As the Polos traveled through Armenia, local people told them that Noah's Ark had rested on Mount Ararat after the flood.

Camel Caravans

As they traveled through the deserts of Iran and Central Asia, the Polos met merchants and their caravans (long lines) of camels, loaded with food stores and valuable goods.

Suspicious Strangers

Wherever the Polos traveled on their way to China, they had to get permission to travel through certain lands from local governors and officials. Many people suspected that the Polos might be spies.

In Konya, eastern Turkey, the Polos passed the beautiful Ince Minareli Madrasa *(Muslim college), built in 1258.*

Erzerum, Turkey

Marco Polo reported that Turkey had many fine cities, rich silver mines and excellent animal-grazing land in the summer months.

Baku, Azerbaijan

On the shores of the Caspian Sea, the Polos saw natural oil wells. The oil was burnt as fuel, or used as skin ointment, and to treat sick horses.

Kashan, Iran

Marco Polo commented on the fine horses he saw in Iran. He also mentioned beautiful, brilliantly-colored ceramics like these (*above*).

•STRANGE VOICES•

Peoples of Central Asia

On his travels, Marco Polo met many different Central Asian peoples. He learned to speak four Asian languages, including Chinese and Turki. These languages were spoken by the Mongols.

Safe Havens

The Polos stayed in "khans," sometimes called "caravanserais." These were public rest-houses, protected by stone walls, where travelers and their animals could find food and water, and sleep safely overnight.

IT TOOK THE POLO FAMILY over three years to travel overland to China. They had to cross rivers and swamps in Iraq, dangerously high mountains in the Hindu Kush, and deserts in Mongolia. Often, they had to wait for the right weather. In winter, mountain passes were blocked with snow, and in summer, the desert sand was so hot it burned travelers' feet. They faced frost-bite, heatstroke, hunger, thirst, and robbers and bandits, too.

Everywhere Marco Polo went, he looked and listened, asked questions and observed the way people lived. He tasted new foods, tried on new clothes, and met new friends.

Travelers had to pass through high mountain ranges and rough terrain. It took 30 days just to cross the Gobi Desert.

Hormuz, Persian Gulf

Here, Marco was astonished to see ships held together with coconut-fiber rope. The local people did not have iron to make nails.

Kerman, Iran

The Polos traveled north from the Gulf, across salt-flats in Iran. The only water they could find was green and too bitter to drink.

Badakhshan, Afghanistan

Marco Polo came to these mountains in Afghanistan to recover from illness, because the air there was so pure and healthy.

•THE DANGER AND DELIGHT OF TRAVEL•

Evil Spirits

Travelers in the desert were frightened of meeting mischievous spirits, called djinns, who wailed and cried in the night. During the day, djinns disguised themselves as people, then led travelers astray so they got lost.

Ghostly Army

Travelers in the desert also reported hearing the noise of a long-dead, ghostly army, marching off to war. They heard the thunder of horses' hooves, and the shouts and cries of battle. This made them very afraid.

Overnight camp

Chinese Borderlands

After crossing the Pamir Mountains, between present-day China and Pakistan, the Polos rode to the oasis at Kashgar.

Khotan, Western China

The Polos passed eerie, deserted towns covered by sand. It was a relief to arrive at Khotan, where sweet grapes and melons grew.

Losing the Way

The wind blew constantly in the desert, choking travelers and covering their tracks. It was very easy to get lost.

•TENTS AND PALACES•

Silken Tent
When he was out hunting, Kublai Khan rested in a splendid tent. It was made of silk and spice-wood, decorated with carved dragons, and ornamented with gold. Inside, it was lined with lion-skins and other expensive furs.

Royal Horses
Marco Polo reported that Kublai Khan owned over 10,000 pure-white horses, which grazed on the steppes near Shangdu. They were treated with great reverence. Only members of Kublai's family could drink their milk.

Kublai and his guests spent their time riding and hunting in the parklands of the palace at Shangdu.

T HE LAST STAGE of the Polos' journey took them across Mongolia to meet the Mongol emperor, Kublai Khan, at his summer palace in Shangdu, on the grassy plains north of Beijing. Kublai greeted the travelers warmly, and held a lavish feast.

Marco reported that he had never seen anything to equal the richness and splendor of Kublai's court. He described Kublai – who was then about 60 years old – as "neither short nor tall, but of medium height. His arms and legs are well fleshed out and shapely. His complexion is fair and ruddy, his eyes black and handsome."

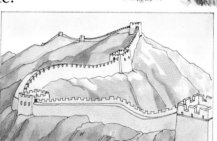

Across China
All along the Silk Road there were busy towns, like Lanchou (modern Lanzhou), where merchants from east and west traded.

Crossing the Wall
Travelers arriving in China along the Silk Road passed close to the remains of the Great Wall. This was built c. 200 BC to keep out invaders.

White Pagoda
On their journey across Mongolia, the Polos probably went to see the famous Wanbuhuayan (White) Pagoda, built around AD 1000.

Enchanters
Magicians and healers from Tibet and Kashmir lived in Kublai Khan's palace at Shangdu. Marco Polo claimed that they used spells to drive away rain-clouds so that the weather around the palace was always fine.

Flying Wine
Marco Polo also claimed that Kublai's Tibetan magicians could make cups full of wine and milk fly through the air at royal feasts, so that drinks were carried to Kublai without the help of any human hands.

Kublai had four chief wives and 22 sons. He had another 25 sons by his unofficial wives. Daughters are not mentioned.

Kublai Khan entertained hundreds of guests at great feasts in the grounds of his summer palace. Some guests were Mongols, others were Chinese.

The Landscape
Mongolia is an arid, cold desert, with few settlements. The Mongolian steppes is a huge area of rolling grasslands and low mountains.

The Emperor's Palace
At Shangdu, Kublai Khan built a magnificent palace of marble and precious stones. He spent three months there each summer.

A Royal Present
When the Polos reached the palace, they presented Kublai Khan with the holy oil they had brought from Jerusalem. He was very pleased.

•KUBLAI KHAN•

Armed Guards
Kublai Khan spent most of his life fighting. (He did not finally conquer all of China until 1279.) Kublai kept control of the lands he had conquered by keeping fierce Mongol soldiers on guard at key points.

Civil Service
Kublai Khan built a new capital city at Khanbalik (modern Beijing). Government officials made sure that people obeyed his laws and paid the taxes he demanded.

Kublai Khan holds court.

THE TERRITORY conquered by warrior Chingiz Khan was divided into four khanates (empires). Kublai ruled the largest, eastern khanate: China, Mongolia, Tibet and nearby lands.

Within his empire, Kublai had absolute power. He introduced Mongol laws and collected heavy taxes, but allowed people to follow their own religion and way of life.

But within half a mile of Kublai's presence, everyone had to speak in hushed voices, so he was not disturbed. They also had to wear white leather slippers, so they would not soil the silken carpets on Kublai's palace floors.

Administration
Kublai Khan appointed governors for all of the provinces in his vast empire. If they disobeyed him, they were killed.

Royal Riders
Relays of riders carried urgent orders. There were staging posts where they could get food and fresh horses along the main roads.

Messengers on Foot
Relay teams also carried royal messages. Each person wore bells, so the next runner could hear them coming and be ready to set off.

•A RULER WITH ABSOLUTE POWER•

Kublai's Lake
Marco Polo described how Kublai Khan gave orders for a huge lake, stocked with fish, to be dug in the palace grounds at Khanbalik.

The Royal Park
According to Marco Polo, the royal palace at Khanbalik was "the largest ever seen." It was surrounded by two strong walls. In between was a park, full of specially-chosen trees, where many beautiful animals lived.

Mongol armies besieged many great cities during Kublai Khan's conquest of China. They camped outside city walls, trying to smash their way in using siege engines, or simply waiting for the trapped inhabitants to starve.

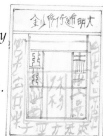

Marco Polo was very impressed by the banknotes he saw being used in China. Paper money was a Mongol invention.

Making Paper
This was a Chinese invention.
1. Cut bamboo from the forest and remove leaves.
2. Boil chopped bamboo with water to make pulp.

3. Spread a thin layer of bamboo pulp on wire mesh to dry.
4. Press and trim the still-damp sheets of pulp.

5. Hang the pressed sheets above an oven to finish drying.
6. Finished paper is stacked neatly, ready for use.

•CHINESE LANDS•

North
Farmers grew wheat, soya beans, and melons on the flat, fertile soils of great river valleys in the north. This was the heartland of China, where Chinese civilization had first flourished.

South
In the warm, wet, south of China, farmers grew rice in flooded fields, known as paddy fields. They bred ducks and geese, and harvested plentiful crops of vegetables such as beans, cabbage-greens, and garlic.

ACCORDING TO MARCO POLO, Kublai Khan was the "mightiest man in the world today, in subjects, territory and treasure."
The densely-populated Chinese lands ruled by Kublai Khan were home to one of the richest, most advanced civilizations in the world. Chinese engineers designed and built wide, paved roads, graceful bridges, thousands of miles of canals and complex irrigation schemes.

Marco Polo admired prosperous cities, fine palaces and temples, beautiful gardens, and many inventions unknown in European lands.

A 13th-century bowl for drinking tea, and a carved lacquer dish and saucer to hold it.

Making Porcelain
1. Chinese craftworkers shaped clay into pots on a potter's wheel.
A specially-fine clay was used to make valuable porcelain.

2. The pots were fired (baked) in a kiln, then allowed to cool. They were painted with delicate patterns – this was a highly-skilled job.

3. The painted pots were fired again after being dipped in glaze – a mixture of chemicals that turned into a thin coating of glass when heated.

Fishing

Fishermen on the Yangtze River used specially-trained cormorants (diving birds) to catch fish for them. A ring around the bird's throat stopped it swallowing its catch.

Mountain Animals

Marco Polo visted Tibet and the neighboring mountain provinces, where he admired the "very handsome" yaks (long-horned cattle).

The Treadmill

Treadmills were machines that used human muscle-power to pump water upwards from streams and ditches.

Irrigation

Chinese engineers dug irrigation channels to bring water to fields, and built sluices and barriers to protect the land from floods.

The Wheelbarrow

Chinese wheelbarrows were invented around AD 200. They were much more efficient than European ones, and easier to push.

•CITY OF HEAVEN•

City of Bridges
Marco Polo said there were 12,000 bridges in Kinsai. This was probably an exaggeration, but since the Chinese were expert bridge-builders, there were no doubt several hundred bridges across the city's rivers, canals, and lake.

Watchmen
Throughout the city, there were big stone towers where citizens could put valuable possessions when a fire broke out. There were also 10 watchmen on duty at each of the main bridges, looking out for dangerous fires.

MARCO POLO reported that the city of Kinsai (present-day Hangzhou) was the "finest and most splendid in the world." Kinsai was the capital of the central region of China, and the largest city in Kublai's empire. Marco visited it several times.

Kinsai had grown rich through trade. Its craftworkers produced exquisite silk fabric, lacquerware, and jewelery. The citizens wore fine clothes and held lavish parties. Marco reported that people ate fish and meat (both expensive luxuries) at the same meal. Kinsai had a huge lake, with summer-houses and palaces all round the shore.

All Kinds of Food
There were ten big markets in Kinsai and countless small, local ones. They sold "everything that could be wished to sustain life."

Sweet and Fragrant
Marco Polo was astonished at all the wonderful fruit on sale in Kinsai, particularly the fragrant pears and sweet, juicy peaches.

Plump and Tasty
Many kinds of fish could be bought in Kinsai markets. The fish were caught in the city's lake, where they grew fat eating rubbish.

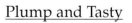

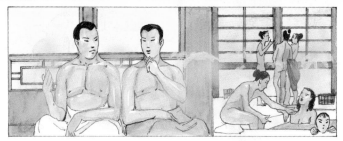

Bathhouses
Marco Polo was impressed by the public bathhouses in Kinsai. Local people bathed daily in cold water, for hygiene and health. There were warm water baths for foreigners who could not stand cold ones.

Rice Wine
Marco Polo also commented on the shops throughout the city that sold spiced rice wine. Local people preferred this to ordinary wine. Fresh batches were made throughout the day and it was very cheap.

Banquets were held by the lake.

Skilled Crafts
According to Marco Polo there were 12 craft guilds in Kinsai, each with 12,000 workshops employing between 10 and 40 people.

Merchants
Kinsai was a trading center, where rich merchants bought and sold silks, medicines and spices from China and the nearby lands.

Wise Men
Some city streets housed scholars who taught reading and writing, or astrologers who cast horoscopes and foretold the future.

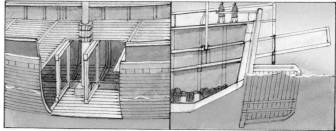

Sailing to India

Marco Polo sailed to India in a Chinese junk. It was much bigger than a European cargo ship. He reported that it could carry 6,000 baskets of pepper. Junks laden with cargo sailed regularly from China to East Africa, too.

Advanced Design

Waterproof bulkheads (compartments) below decks made junks very hard to sink. Their masts and sails were arranged to catch the maximum amount of wind, and they were steered by a rudder at the stern (back).

MARCO'S FATHER and uncle seem to have spent most of their time in China working as traders, but Marco was sent on long journeys to distant parts of Kublai's empire as a messenger, or perhaps a spy. He visited many remote regions, including Tibet, Burma (present-day Myanmar), Bengal (present-day Bangladesh), and Laos – where he marveled at people who coated their teeth with solid gold and who covered their bodies with tattoos.

On his journeys, Marco met other travelers who told him tales of amazing things they had seen. Some of these travelers' tales may have been exaggerated, but many of them were true.

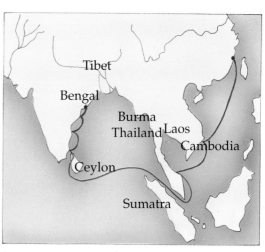

Marco spent many years traveling in South-East Asia. In his book he described many of the countries he visited. These descriptions are a valuable historical record.

Pearl Fishers

Off the coasts of Ceylon and eastern India, Marco Polo watched divers search underwater for oysters containing pearls.

War Elephants

In Cambodia, Marco Polo heard stories of King Jayavarman. He paid Kublai Khan tribute of war elephants – and had 326 children.

Tales of Australia

In the Spice Islands, Marco Polo met sailors who spoke of a mysterious southern land. It was probably Australia, unknown to Europeans then.

Buddha's Tooth

In Ceylon (present-day Sri Lanka), Marco Polo met Buddhist monks. They told him they had sent Kublai Khan holy relics, such as the Buddha's tooth.

Temple Dancers

In India, Marco Polo admired the young women who danced in front of statues of gods and goddesses in Hindu temples. They also offered the statues food and garlands of flowers.

In Burma, Marco Polo traveled past Buddhist temples and gold-covered stupas (Buddhist shrines) like this one at Mingalazedi.

Money Shells

In Thailand, Marco Polo saw cowrie shells being collected. They were used instead of money by traders in many Asian lands.

Unicorns

In Sumatra, Indonesia, Marco described "very ugly brutes," which he said were unicorns. They were probably black rhinoceroses.

Men with Tails

In Sumatra, Marco Polo saw "men with tails." In fact, they were orangutans, a species of ape that lives in the rainforests there.

Friends or Strangers
When the Polos arrived back in Venice, dirty and shabby, no one recognized them. They ripped open the seams of their Mongol-style clothes to reveal the jewels they had hidden inside and at last everyone believed them.

Welcome Home
Marco and his father arranged a great feast. Everyone welcomed them home. Their family was very relieved – they thought that Marco, his father and his uncle had died on their travels many years before.

AFTER TRAVELING in the East for over 20 years, the Polos wanted to go home. Marco was nearing 40 and his father and uncle were old men. But they could not leave China without Kublai Khan's permission. How could they persuade him to let them go?

By great good fortune, a troop of soldiers, courtiers and servants were getting ready to leave Kublai's court, as escorts to a Mongol princess traveling to marry a ruler in the Middle East. The overland route was blocked by war, so the Polos volunteered to act as guides for the journey by sea. They set off in 1292 and finally reached Venice in 1295.

The Polos finally returned home after over 24 years.

The Journey Home
When the Polos left with the princess, Kublai Khan gave them gold tokens that ordered his subjects to give them food and provisions.

A Fleet of Ships
The Mongol princess, Kokachin, and her servants, together with the Polos, sailed in a fleet of 14 ships around India to the Persian Gulf.

The Voyage
The voyage took 18 months and was full of dangers. Marco said that out of 700 people on board, only 117 survived.

Stories in Prison
In 1298, Venice went to war with Genoa. Marco was captured and put in prison. There, he met a writer called Rustichello of Pisa. To pass the time, he told Rustichello stories about his travels. Rustichello then wrote them down.

Best-Seller
Rustichello turned Marco Polo's stories into a book. It soon became very popular and was translated into many different languages. Everyone enjoyed listening to the story of Marco's amazing adventures.

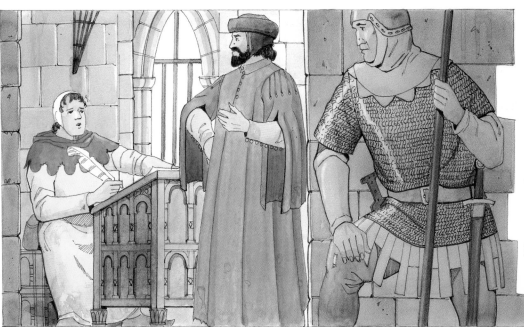

Marco Polo may have exaggerated some of his adventures to make himself appear brave and glamorous, and Rustichello may have added some extra, imaginary episodes of his own. He had written mostly romances before. But historians have checked many of the details about people and places that are mentioned in the book. It seems as if most of Marco's story is probably true.

Kokachin Delivered Safely
The Polos and Princess Kokachin were among the survivors. The Polos took her to meet her bridegroom on the borders of Iran.

Towards the Black Sea
For the next nine months, the Polos continued their journey overland, traveling westwards to the shores of the Black Sea.

Home at Last
For the final stage of their journey, the Polos sailed by ship from the Black Sea port of Trebizond (modern Trabzon) then on to Venice.

WE KNOW very little about the last years of Marco Polo's life, after he was set free from prison in 1299. Only two pieces of evidence survive. One is a manuscript which calls him by his nickname, "Il Milione" (Mr. Million). We do not know why he was called this – perhaps because of his boastful talk about his travels, perhaps because of the treasures he brought home with him. The second, and last, piece of evidence is Marco's will, made shortly before his death in 1324. In this, he mentions that he has three daughters, and leaves them a substantial amount of money – though not an enormous fortune. This suggests that Marco had perhaps exaggerated the amount of treasures he had brought back with him to Venice. In his will, Marco also mentions his servant, Peter, who came from the Tatars (a Mongol tribe). Marco gives instructions that when he dies, Peter should be set free.

MARCO POLO, his father, and his uncle, were among the first to make the difficult and dangerous journey right along the Silk Road. But they were also among the last to do so for almost 500 years.

IN 1320, a Christian missionary, Fra Odoric of Pordenone, set out for China hoping to spread the Christian faith. We do not know whether he ever met Marco Polo, or knew of Marco's book. If he had read it, he would have discovered from Marco's descriptions that very few people in Asia knew about Christianity in the 1260s or 1270s. But by 1307, the situation had changed. In that year, the Pope appointed the first Roman Catholic Bishop of Beijing. This suggests there was a sizeable Christian community living there, and that several Christian missionaries may have been working in northern China in Marco Polo's time. In the book he wrote around 1330 about his journey to China, Odoric remarked, "there are now many people in Venice who have visited Kinsai."

THE LAST MEDIEVAL European we know about who visited China was another Italian merchant, named Francesco Balducci Pegolotti. He went there in about 1340 and wrote a guide for other travelers called *The Merchants' Handbook*. It is not as entertaining and enjoyable as Marco Polo's book, but Pegolotti does make one interesting comment: "the road from the Black Sea to China is now perfectly safe, by day or by night."

But this period of peaceful and successful travel did not last long. In 1368 the Chinese people rebelled against their Mongol rulers, drove them out of the country, and set up a new ruling family of their own. Under these new rulers – called the Ming Dynasty – foreigners were not welcome to visit China. Brave, adventurous, profitable journeys, like the one pioneered by Marco Polo and his family, would not again be possible for hundreds of years.

Barter
To exchange goods of equal value.

Bronze
A mixture of copper and tin, used to make decorative objects, containers, and ceremonial swords.

Bulkheads
Compartments. Used especially to describe storage areas in ships.

Caravans
Herds of specially-trained camels, used to carry heavy loads for long distances over dry or desert land.

Caravanserai
See "Khan (ii)" (*below*).

Ceramics
Items made from clay, especially pottery, tiles, and porcelain.

Empire
Many nations joined together under the rule of a single leader called an emperor.

Ewer
Water jug.

Exotic
Coming from faraway lands.

Frost-bite
Damage to skin (especially nose, fingers, and toes) caused by extreme cold.

Glazed
Covered with a shiny surface layer.

Heatstroke
Illness caused by too much exposure to hot sun. Sufferers have a raised temperature and a severe headache.

Khan (i)
Mongol word for ruler.

Khan (ii)
Public rest-house where travelers and their animals could stay safely overnight. Also called a "caravanserai."

Khanate
Lands ruled by a Khan.

Kumiz
Alcoholic drink made by Mongols from mares' milk.

Mongols
Nomad peoples who lived in Central Asia and present-day Mongolia. They were brave fighters and expert horse-riders. In the 13th century they conquered a vast empire, led by Chingiz and Kublai Khan.

Mosque
Building where Muslims go to pray and listen to readings from the Muslim holy book, the Qur'an (Koran).

Nomads
People who move their homes from place to place, in search of food and water for themselves and, sometimes, their herds of animals.

Porcelain
Very fine, white, hard pottery, made from a special kind of clay.

Sluice
An underwater gate that regulates the flow of water passing through it.

Steppes
Vast, flat grasslands in Central Asia and the Far East. The steppes were home to the Mongols and their herds of horses, sheep, and goats.

Yurt
Mongol tent, made of felt on a wooden frame.

INDEX